How Do You Spell

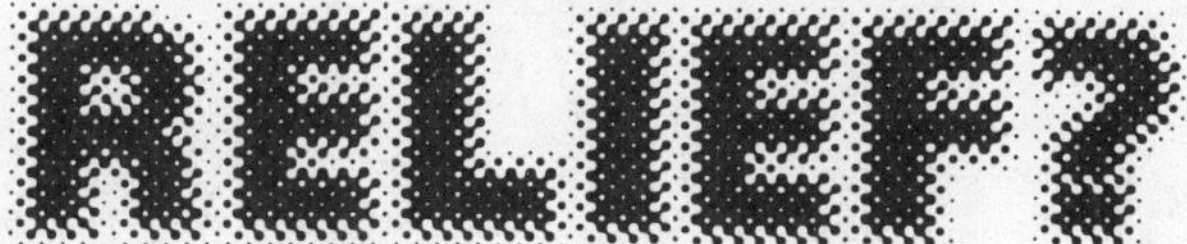

Lucile H. Jones

Pacific Press Publishing Association
Boise, Idaho
Montemorelos, Nuevo Leon, Mexico
Oshawa, Ontario, Canada

Edited by D. E. Mansell
Designed by Tim Larson
Cover photo by Duane Tank
Type: 10/12 Century Schoolbook

First Printing 1986

Library of Congress Cataloging in Publication Data

Jones, Lucile H., 1910-
   How do you spell relief?

   Bibliography: p.
   1. Health. 2. Christian life—1960-
I. Title
RA776.J695   1986   613   85-25872
ISBN 0-8163-0631-1

Contents

Dedication

Lovingly dedicated to my husband, Carl Trainer Jones, whose encouragement, patience, and suggestions enabled me to write this book.

Chapter 1

I Spell It—EXERCISE

Fifty-eight-year-old Dick Kegley dropped into his chair. He coughed and wheezed. The miserable expression on his pale face reflected the stress of asthma and serious allergies.

He got up and sauntered around his car sales lot, taking the opportunity to breath as deeply as he could. This gave him a few minutes' relief.

At night his wife, Margaret, propped him up in bed with two or three pillows. As his condition worsened, time and again she had to call the doctor, who urged her, "Get him to the hospital at once. I'll meet you at the emergency room." Always she wondered, "Can I get him there in time?"

After a short stay in the hospital Dick would return home to await the next frightening episode. But the questions haunted him, "When will it happen again?" and "Will I survive the next attack?"

Gradually an idea crept into Dick's thinking: all these runners who pass here every day seem to be in fine fettle! As he talked with some of them and heard their stories of improved digestion, lowered blood pressure, and brighter mental outlook, he ventured to ask Margaret, "Do you think running could help me?"

"It just might, if you think you are able. But first, better check with Dr. Hale."

A few days later with the doctor's approval Dick began running just a couple of blocks, or a little more on his better days. "Come on, Margaret, run with me," he invited her. "I enjoy every flower, bird, and pet along the road. My run is the highlight of my day."

As he continued to run a little farther each day, his strength increased, his problems diminished, and he actually felt like reading several hours every evening. Jogging became exciting, because, as he explains, "Today I can read material which I have read many times, but see things in it that I never saw there before."

As Dick increased his jogging mileage, he reached his ideal weight. His stronger heart beat more slowly, resting between beats. He smiles now as he declares, "The allergies, asthma, and medicines are gone! My blood pressure is 120/70. My doctor says that's excellent. Running has built up my resistance too."

Now, six years and sixty trophies later, Dick Kegley lives vigorously instead of just existing. With increased strength and endurance he easily takes a fifty-mile run. He even ran 1100 miles from his home in College Place, Washington, to Loma Linda, California. In April 1984 at the New Astley Belt six-day race he broke his own 1983 world record and was again acclaimed long-distance champion runner of the world for men sixty years and over!

Of course, you don't have to be fifty-eight and you don't have to have asthma or allergies to discover what a good exercise program can do for you. College students find that even moderate physical activity helps them break the tension and stress they are under as a result of constant study, tests, and term papers.

Many physicians now prescribe walking, swimming, bowling, and especially golf, for those who need relief from tensions and anxieties.

Physiologists have found that, when you exercise, your bone marrow makes red cells at a faster rate. This is significant because red blood cells carry fresh oxygen to your brain and all parts of your body. In addition to improving the quality of your blood, exercise hastens the flow of lymph, removing the waste products that would make you feel sluggish.

Not only running but other simple exercises can help you to feel better. If you sit at your work, you may find that shrugging then relaxing your shoulders several times is an easy way to relieve tension, pain, and headaches. Getting up and walking around at least once every hour is important to prevent blood clots.

Next time you are up-tight, try taking a brisk walk. Instead of becoming more tired and tense, you will find yourself unwinding. Nathan Pritikin explains that inactive muscles build up strong electrical charges that keep you awake, but when you exercise "you can discharge those voltages and muscles relax. Dissipating those electrical charges in the muscles is precisely what tranquilizers do."

We need to balance our emotions with motion. How can you do that?

Suppose you become angry or upset at your spouse or someone else. Instead of fighting and saying harsh words you will later regret, go out and play a game of tennis together. This will use up the excess electrical charges your anger has produced, calm your emotions, and as a result, strengthen your relationship. One Christian writer even suggests that if you are angry you might get more good out of chopping a load of wood than by sitting through a prayer meeting.

Whether you choose to run, jog, walk, bike, golf, or just work in your garden, you will find enjoyable activity an excellent way to spell—*relief!*

Chapter 2

I Spell It—FRESH AIR

Remember the feel of the cold air on your face when you were younger on those crisp winter evenings when your skates sped over the ice? The invigorating effect of the fresh air sent oxygen-loaded blood surging to every cell of your body. It deepened your breathing, quickened your heartbeat, and sharpened your brain.

Or maybe you recall a lovely spring day on a tropical beach—the sound of the crashing waves, the taste of the salty spray? As you jumped the waves or rode the surf, the moist, fresh air bathed your cheeks and your whole body thrilled with the joy of renewed energy.

Perhaps on an early summer evening you became so enchanted working with your flowers and garden—remember the fragrance of the roses, the mint, and the strawberries; the buzz of the bees on the open blossoms; the song of the meadowlark—that you didn't notice the sun had set. You kept right on working until you could no longer tell the weeds from the plants.

All of these activities in the wide out-of-doors fill me with the wish that I could just keep on doing them forever, and never have to stop. It's so much fun! I love the fragrance, sound, and color of living things—the feel of the cool, fresh air!

Without the air you couldn't enjoy the comradeship

of laughter as you skate, the sound of the pounding surf as you swim, the hum of the bees, nor the song of the birds as you work.

You would have to get along without those smells of luscious berries and mint, the fragrance of roses and locust blossoms, because it is the air that carries these aromas to your olfactory nerves. But more than this— you would have no energy to enjoy these things if there were no oxygen in the air to "burn" your food.

Can you appreciate God's wisdom in giving us the air on the second day of Creation? He had it all ready and waiting for the fragrance of the flowers on the third day, the song of the birds on the fifth, the sense of smell for the animals on the sixth, and ready for Eve to hear Adam say, "I love you," that Friday afternoon.

If you are a shallow breather, you limit the intake of oxygen needed to keep your brain alert, and you may be missing the lift you could have that chases away depression.

I know a busy homemaker who reminds herself to "breathe deeply" by pasting small notices over her kitchen deck, at the sink, and on her bathroom mirror.

If you practice breathing deeply, it can soothe your nerves and help you to be composed and serene. When you feel irritated or annoyed, it is a good practice to stop and take a few deep breaths while you think twice.

You should get outside for a while every day, and as you do so, you will discover that plenty of fresh air will stimulate your circulation, improve your digestion, and help you to sleep better. When you are sick, rest in the fresh air will help to speed your recovery.

You notice we have been talking about pure, fresh air. Not all air is pure or fresh. Researchers at Cornell University Medical School recently discovered that people who jogged for half an hour along a busy New

York highway had carbon monoxide levels in their blood as high as that in persons who smoke ten to twenty cigarettes a day. Breathing carbon monoxide is dangerous because the molecules of this compound attach themselves to the hemoglobin in your blood, which carries oxygen to the rest of your body. Anything that inhibits oxygen's getting to your cells is life-threatening to some degree.

Your body also needs air in motion to evaporate perspiration that collects on the surface of your skin. Such evaporation keeps you comfortable and controls your body temperature. While high humidity retards evaporation and makes you feel hot, sticky, drowsy, and even depressed, it is not best for the air in your home to be too dry. If it is, the lining of your respiratory tract can become irritated and susceptible to infection.

Cold air stimulates, but overexposure can be dangerous because it raises your blood pressure and decreases the number of white cells—an important part of your immune system.

Deep breathing while maintaining good posture gets plenty of oxygen down into the less accessible corners of your lungs and kills the germs that may be hiding there.

Step outside into the fresh air—inhale—exhale—deeply—repeat this exercise to spell—*relief!*

Chapter 3

I Spell It—SUNSHINE

"Look out your kitchen window," my neighbor called on the phone.

There in the west a majestic sunset spread in layers of brilliant orange and red tinged with gold and pink. I watched the dogwood in my backyard become a silhouette, while the mums and snapdragons turned to clumps of gray and black.

Color is one of the blessings of sunshine. Try to imagine a rainbow in simple black and white! Can you visualize a colorless peacock! Or daffodils that were only shades of grey! And how would you like to have hair, eyes, and lips that had no hue? What a dull world this would be with no red for apples, yellow for daisies, blue for the sky, or green for the grass! Ugh! How horrid!

But sunlight gives much more than color to our world. In the spring it melts the snow to make the streams flow again. It awakens hibernating animals and triggers the nesting hormone in birds. In summer it makes our gardens grow. In fruit it changes starch to sugar and in grains, sugar to starch.

The warmth of the sun heats the volatile oils present in flowers and scatters the perfume—rich and fragrant—through air currents that are set in motion by the sun's rays.

Suppose sunlight didn't kill germs. Think of the mold, decay, and disease we would have! Man would have perished from the earth long ago, but for sunlight. Sunshine is one of nature's greatest healing agencies. This is the reason we need an abundance of it in every room, but especially our bedrooms when we are sick.

Dr. Lawrence P. Garrod, professor of bacteriology at the University of London, found that the dust under the bed and in the dark corners of hospital rooms was loaded with disease-producing bacteria, but dust from near the window or on the windowsill had none. He says we have to recognize that ordinary daylight, even on a cloudy day in winter, does kill bacteria.

When Marty, a friend of mine, came over one day, I noticed that her skin, usually splotched with psoriasis lesions, looked soft and pink. She explained, "I've been taking sunbaths." Apparently sunlight was beneficial in her case. Later she purchased a sunlamp to use when the weather was bad.

But too much sunlight can produce what some consider undesirable effects. Of the seven children in my parents' family, I inherited freckles. As a child I didn't spend much time in front of the mirror, but as I grew older, I became more concerned. But then, one day I discovered that the Bible says that a person with freckles is "clean." See Leviticus 13:39. Well, at least that made me feel better.

Today it is possible to generate electricity from sunlight by using solar cells. With these cells you can charge up your battery in the daytime and use it at night for lighting or electrical appliances.

It has been observed that people who have been in the sun a reasonable time are usually more alert, happy, and energetic than those who sit in the shade trying to look beautiful. Perhaps, like solar cells, these people convert sunlight into body energy.

Among its other blessings, sunshine helps in the formation of vitamin D which, in turn, improves the utilization of calcium to make teeth and bones stronger. For this reason it is especially beneficial in healing bone fracture. This increased vitamin D with better calcium utilization builds teeth that are more resistant to decay. Sadly, in a few areas of our country where there is a large percentage of cloudy, misty, or smoggy days, many young people already have false teeth.

Some people report that for them sunshine acts like a tranquilizer and improves their sleep. It also helps to soothe the aching of arthritic joints. Other benefits which you may not notice are that it increases liver function, improves the utilization of oxygen in your body cells, and increases the number of the germ-fighting white blood cells.

An observant nurse in England cared for jaundiced premature babies in the hospital nursery. Because of their premature condition they lacked an enzyme which the liver produces that gets rid of bilirubin. This substance is formed in the normal process of red blood cells breaking down, but the bilirubin in these little "premies" accumulates and turns the skin yellow. But this is not all that it does. The worst part is that it damages the brain and sometimes even causes death. The nurse I was telling you about noticed and reported that the babies nearest the window, where they got more light, showed greater improvement than those farther back in the nursery. Subsequent research proved that her observation was valid. Now, each year, thousands of premature infants in the United States are treated successfully with light to prevent or cure jaundice.

A little sunshine is good—but a lot is *not* better! If you are a blond, light-complexioned and blue-eyed, you need to take extra precautions against getting sunburn. Perhaps you would profit by using a good sunscreen lotion. While it may be true that sunbathing can reduce stress and has many healing properties, it can be dangerous. Persisted in, it may even cause skin cancer. So, if you are going to sunbathe, begin cautiously, and progress gradually, and don't overdo it.

Some of my friends like to take walks in the evening. But that's not for me. My husband, Carl, and I schedule our walks in the morning just as the sun sends its glowing fingers above the Blue Mountains of eastern Washington state. As it climbs higher, so do our spirits. It gives us a great feeling of well-being and stimulates our appetites so that by the time we get home we're ready for a nourishing breakfast.

Try wise use of sunshine in your home and on your body to spell—*relief!*

Chapter 4

I Spell It—TEMPERANCE

I welcomed Jeanne at my door, but she seemed uneasy, jittery, and in no state to rest for even a minute. "Can you go for a ride?" she pleaded.

The desperation in her voice told me that I must go.

She drove to a nearby park, then turning to me begged, "Talk, just talk to me! I haven't smoked a cigarette all day!"

"Good for you!" I gave her a pat on her shoulder. "That's great!" I complimented her.

Jeanne loved children—her three boys, her fifth-grade pupils, the youngsters in the ball teams she coached after school, and her Sunday School class.

If she were the only one to be affected by the hundreds of chemicals in her cigarette smoke that would be one thing. But as a mother and teacher she must set a good example for these youth! Unless she did, they could end up being among the thousands killed by smoking each year as victims of cancer and heart disease. She couldn't do that to her boys and girls!

In addition, she realized that her smoking could cause even nonsmokers in the same room with her to have eye problems, headaches, coughs, and sneezes, and even serious lung conditions.

The revolting smell of secondhand tobacco saturated

her hair and clothes after every lunch break. Everybody knew Jeanne smoked. She had tried to hide nothing. "At least I'm honest about it," she consoled herself.

And yet she felt responsible for the girls in her Sunday School class. She was doing her best to guide them by right principles and example—or was she? Not altogether, she wasn't. Soon these girls would be young mothers. If they smoked, their babies would tend to be smaller, more sickly, contract flu and pneumonia more easily, and would be more likely to die during their first year of life. She also knew that many other pregnancies would terminate in miscarriages or stillbirths. No! she was not going to exert that kind of influence on her girls!

She and I talked about what she could do to give up the tobacco habit. Among other things, she resolved not to sit in a smoke-saturated chair to read the evening paper, but instead to go on a bike ride or take a walk at the times she usually smoked. She decided to drink lots of water to replace coffee, tea, colas, and alcoholic drinks which I told her intensify the craving for cigarettes.

I encouraged her to skip fried or highly spiced foods, as well as those high in sugar content. Another helpful practice would be to go on an entirely fruit and fruit-juice diet for the first twenty-four hours to get rid of the nicotine in her body and, in addition, take a warm shower morning and evening to get it off her skin surface.

Since the severe craving for tobacco comes in attacks that last only about three and one half minutes, she could at such times briefly splash cold water on her face or take a short run outside to divert her attention from her cravings.

Jeanne decided to get her pupils into outdoor

recreation and away from cigarettes, feeling this would help them later to build defenses against the marijuana habit. To reinforce this she shared with them the *Listen* magazine and other publications that warn against drugs that can weaken resistance to disease and precipitate serious mental problems.

As Jeanne led her students and children in the right direction, she discovered that her willpower increased and her desire to smoke decreased. I urged her to call and talk with me any time she needed help. Every day, when she reported to me on her progress, I complimented and encouraged her. Together we prayed for continued success. It took *work—hard work*! But Jeanne's determination and God's power completely changed her life from that of a tobacco slave to a beautiful role model for the youth who admired her happy buoyant personality. If you need help to break the smoking habit, call the local Seventh-day Adventist pastor or hospital chaplain and inquire about the Five-Day Plan to Stop Smoking.

Bob Welch, Los Angeles Dodgers' pitcher, found that drinking almost brought his career to a halt. Alcoholism, like the marijuana habit, fools its victims into thinking they are smarter and their reflexes faster. The truth, so clear to everyone around them, is that it has the opposite effect. Their sluggish brains and silly behavior make them dangerous drivers or even unsafe pedestrians. Frequently their personalities become so ugly their friends prefer not to be with them.

Bob didn't realize how adversely alcohol was affecting him. He imagined his friends had turned against him, and he became angry at them. His irrational behavior reached the point that it became an embarrassment to his teammates. One day a friend took him to dinner. After the meal Bob's friend cautiously told him how he, himself, had gotten the victory over alcoholism at a rehabilitation center, The Meadows, in Arizona. Fortunately for Bob and the Dodgers, he took his friend's advice and went to The Meadows for treatment.

To keep fit Bob eats less meat than he formerly did and runs about fifteen miles a week, in addition to his regular team workouts. Now he tells other young people the truth: "Alcohol clouds your brain. You can't think straight if you're drunk." He beams when he confesses, "One of the greatest joys of being sober is waking up in the morning and really feeling great. It's a joy being able to face problems instead of running from them."

If you have an alcohol problem call the AA (Alcoholics Anonymous) organization listed in your telephone book. They will help you.

Getting off tobacco, alcohol, and other drugs is a great way to spell—*relief!*

Chapter 5

I Spell It—REST

"Mrs. Jones, I never have seen you walk. You always run," a fellow worker remarked after watching me for five years.

"Oh, am I really that bad?" I wondered. I decided to check up on myself, fearing he might be right. He *was* right! I tended to hurry from one self-imposed task to another, to rush from one tiring day to the next.

One day I was on my way to the store, when I caught myself walking fast. When I realized what I was doing, I gave myself a good lecture: "Slow down, Lucile. You don't have to hurry this much! You can stop, look, and listen. Enjoy this day!"

I needed to remember to take time to live, time to think, time to smile, and time to play—time for just plain fun! I should have slowed down years ago. But the strange thing is that I didn't realize what I was missing, rushing around as fast as I did, nor how much blood pressure and stress I was adding to the normal wear and tear of living.

One day I decided to relax a few minutes once or twice a day and discovered that it can pay high dividends in reduced stress, increased efficiency, and greater endurance. Actually, catnaps are preferable because one- or two-hour sleeps can upset your body's twenty-four-hour rhythm.

Shakespeare aptly referred to the "sleep that knits up the ravelled sleeve of care." It is then that your skeletal muscles, heart muscle, kidneys, bone marrow, stomach lining, and brain cells all are restored. During sleep your brain files recent information, thus making space for incoming data.

You can't replace your brain like a car battery, but you can recharge it through sleep. Some researchers believe that sleep even reinforces your character structure and that dreaming is necessary for you to maintain good mental health.

Children need an abundance of sleep, for it is then that their muscles and bones have the best chance to grow. Sleep is also good for adults. If you sprain an ankle, cut yourself, or break a bone, it will heal faster with extra sleep. Adequate sleep builds resistance to germs. That is why you get over colds sooner, if you rest more.

Another form of resistance that builds up during periods of rest is resistance to temptation. A respected Bible teacher once counseled his students: "Never make a major decision late at night. Wait until the next morning when you are rested and your mind is clear."

Although you may not realize it, you dream about every ninety minutes while you sleep. Dreams seem to be an important factor in rapid learning and developing a good memory.

How much sleep do you need? You may feel you don't need as much as the average person, but your spouse probably could tell you that your disposition is the sweetest and you're the nicest to live with when you have from seven to nine hours of sleep regularly. A sleepy person simply is not at his best, and the sleepier he is, the less effective will be his relationships and his productivity.

During World War II English workers labored at their job twelve hours a day for seven days a week. Their very lives depended on producing defense materials. But public health authorities discovered that workers with so little rest became inefficient. After trying everything else, management finally tried cutting back from eighty-four to sixty hours a week. Strangely, production improved. Then they dropped the work load to forty-six hours, and finally even lower. Each diminution of the number of working hours increased production. In one factory workers reached their peak when they stayed at their jobs only forty-three and a half hours a week.

This reinforces the truth that God made man to function best on one day of rest each week. Forty-three and a half hours would be five, eight-hour days and about one more half day for work. That leaves the other half of the sixth day for us to get ready for the seventh, the Sabbath—ready in mind and body, so we can truly "rest in the Lord."

Jinny and Ted found out the hard way that caring for our bodies is important. As newlyweds, they thrilled at the thought of working together in an overseas mission. Both, having been trained for the work in which they were to engage, could scarcely wait to start packing. But their physical examination revealed that Jinny was unfit for the assignment. She was totally unsuited physically and emotionally for the job.

Heartsick, she confessed that throughout her college years she had carried a heavy load with far too little rest. This took its toll, and the price she paid was failure to realize her greatest ambition—serving in the mission field.

If you have a hard time getting to sleep, darken your room, adjust the temperature, turn off all sounds, take a warm shower, and establish a regular bedtime. Frequently these help.

Here's the way Dr. O. A. Battista, a research chemist, clears his brain for sleep. "My personal routine," he says "is to imagine a wastebasket beside the bed, and as each cluttering thought comes to mind, I mentally discard it by tossing it into the wastebasket. As soon as the basket is full and my mind is empty, I'm off to slumberland."

A Christian writer says that when she has difficulty sleeping, she starts with "A" and quotes a Bible text that begins with each letter of the alphabet until she gets to "Z"—or "ZZZZ-Z-Z-Z," whichever comes first.

Drifting into dreamland on an eight-hour cruise is a good way to spell—*relief!*

Chapter 6

I Spell It—DIET

"Lose fifty pounds overnight!

"Just like magic! By following these twenty-seven simple steps you will melt pounds and inches like butter in a frying pan. Just send us $50 and your complete measurements, birthdate, etc."

Now, isn't that wonderful? Wouldn't you like to take advantage of this unbelievable offer?

Well, it *is* unbelievable! And *you better believe it*! The only thing the people lost who answered that advertisement was their $50.

Can you spot a quack or unreliable information? Here are a few pointers:

1. An out-of-town person.
2. Use of testimonials.
3. Fee *before* service.
4. Exorbitant claims, often cures.
5. Secrecy.
6. Claims of persecution by medical authorities.

Some wag has put it this way: When you see a quack—duck!

A safe way to lose pounds in order to reach your ideal weight is to check your diet with the *Dietary Guidelines for Americans* published by the United States Department of Health and Human Services, and probably found in your local library. It recommends that you—

1. *Maintain Ideal Weight*—usually about what you weighed when 20 to 25 years old. The best way to make sure you are on a good program is to get your doctor to help you plan one that includes diet and exercise to help you lose not more than two pounds a week. You may find help in eating slowly, taking smaller servings, and avoiding seconds. A slimmer figure usually means a better self-concept, less work for your heart, and less stress on your joints.

2. *Eat a Variety of Foods Daily*. First we think of fruit. Did you ever wonder whether an apple a day really does help to keep the doctor away? To check on this, student volunteers at Michigan State University ate apples during the first and second quarters of three academic years. At the end of the experiment the record showed they had better general health and had made fewer clinic calls for treatment of upper respiratory infections and tension-pressure disorders than expected on the basis of the entire student body.

Vegetables are another important group of foods. Although people once thought tomatoes and potatoes were poisonous, they have become some of our most wholesome and popular vegetables. We need green, leafy vegetables for vitamins, minerals, and roughage. The cruciferous vegetables—cabbage, Brussels sprouts, cauliflower and broccoli—are believed by some researchers to offer resistance to cancer. The whole grains and legumes—peas, beans, lentils, etc.—supply excellent fiber, as well as good-quality protein. Of course you will need adequate milk and other protein foods to promote growth and antibody formation.

3. *Avoid Too Much Fat, Especially Saturated Fats and Cholesterol*. If you are wondering how you can do this, you might try some of the new low-fat, low-calorie vegetable meat analogs. The taste, texture, and versa-

tility of these products may surprise you. They have excellent nutrition and are easy to use. They contain no bones or feathers and do not shrink.

4. *Eat Food With Adequate Starch and Fiber.* Whole grains and legumes provide some of our best sources of fiber, an important factor for sweeping away the cholesterol and waste products in the intestines. The shorter time food lies in contact with the intestinal lining seems to lessen the susceptibility to cancer of the colon.

5. *Avoid Too Much Sugar.* The average American uses over 130 pounds of sugar per year. What is wrong with sugar? Too much sugar increases dental decay and overworks the pancreas. It also adds pounds. An interesting study on rats showed that those that were put on the popular American diet, including coffee, spices, sweets, and highly refined food, drank five times as much alcohol as those on the control human diet of fruits, grains, legumes, nuts, and milk.

If you avoid the snack bar you may not only cut your dental bills, but you will also improve your resistance to disease. The reason for this is simple: The more sugar you use, the more you lessen the ability of your white blood cells to fight germs.

Did you ever hear of candy criminals? Studies have shown that children's behavior patterns definitely improve with a good diet containing few sweets. Some people eat a great many sweets and, as a result, become mentally unbalanced and commit serious crimes.

6. *Avoid Too Much Sodium.* Simply by cutting down on plain table salt may help you lower your blood pressure and better protect your heart.

With these guidelines you can wisely choose a healthful diet.

Your menu can spell—*relief!*

Chapter 7

I Spell It—WATER

When Terry knocked at our door I thought he had come on business. He surprised me when he took a comfortable chair, leaned back, and rested his feet on a stool.

He drew a deep breath and sighed, "I'm so tired. I had a bad time on that trip to the convention last week. The water was awful. I just couldn't drink it. Then we got terrible news of a family tragedy. The shock threw me into a severe diarrhea attack that kept worsening until I was so dehydrated I collapsed on the floor—my mind so fuzzy and my mouth so dry I couldn't talk."

Fortunately Terry's wife took over and called a doctor, who sent him by ambulance to the hospital. In the emergency room the doctor began fluids by intravenous—and by mouth when Terry was able to drink.

"After four hours and replaced fluids I was OK," he told me. Then he confessed, "Since that episode I've been drinking water whether I like it or not."

Do you enjoy the benefits of six to eight glasses of pure water every day?

Water is imperative for all living things. "Birds fly to it. Animals run to it. Babies cry for it." But too many adults forget to drink water. They substitute coffee, tea, or cola drinks. These popular drinks contain too much sugar and empty calories. Many contain caffeine, which speeds up your heart, raises your blood pressure, promotes blood clots, and increases acid in your stomach. The sugar in pop also slows the rate at which the water in your drink can be absorbed.

Because we eliminate so much liquid through our kidneys, skin, lungs, and colon, we need to drink more than most of us do.

"Oh, I drink ten or twelve times a day at the drinking fountain," you say?

That's a good start, but it isn't equivalent to six glasses. A friend of mine went to the fountain, took a big sip of water, then spit into a glass. Would you guess how many sips it takes to make one glassful? Fifteen to twenty—depending upon the size of your sip!

Water is more than just a thirst-quencher. It is the mainstream of your life—a solvent and dispersion medium for nutrients, electrolytes (minerals, mainly sodium and potassium), and waste products.

Why do we need so much water? To make tears, saliva, other digestive juices, blood, and lymph. Even your brain cells are about 79 percent fluid. If you have a fever, frequent drinks of water will help to make you more comfortable and lower your temperature.

Yet too much water can be harmful. One woman visiting in our community became so weak she fainted. Her friends took her to the hospital, and when she regained consciousness the doctor asked her a few questions. She revealed that the only thing she had done differently from usual was to drink a lot of water.

"How much?" he wanted to know.

"Oh, several gallons," she admitted. She had read that most Americans don't drink enough water and consequently made sure she had plenty. In ignorance she had drunk so much that she dangerously depleted the electrolytes so important for regulating her heartbeat, kidney function, and mental alertness.

Water on the outside of your body is almost as important as on the inside. Alternate hot and cold showers do much more than to remove the oils and dirt from your skin. They speed up circulation, helping you to think more clearly. They also make your muscles more flexible and help your whole digestive system work better.

As a first-aid instructor, I learned that water often is the first thing to reach for in an emergency. If you sprain your ankle, place it in cold water immediately, and off and on during the first twenty-four hours. This helps to keep it from swelling and eases the pain.

Or if you burn yourself, submerge the burned area in very cold, even ice water, at once. Again this eases the pain, stops tissue destruction, and speeds healing.

A hot foot bath is an excellent means of relieving a headache by dilating the blood vessels in the feet and drawing the blood away from the head. Hot water often can be used for lessening pain, such as in arthritic joints or an aching back. Never use hot water for appendicitis, however.

Among other blessings, water is the most economical way of generating electricity. Did you know that it takes about 650 gallons of water to make the steel for one bicycle or 200 gallons to make the rubber in one car tire? Our food production rises or falls due to the rainfall, for it takes about 140 gallons of water to raise enough wheat to make one loaf of bread.

Beauty is another blessing of water. When did you last enjoy a colorful rainbow-crowned waterfall? The moonlight magic of a silver thaw? The dewdrop diamonds on your lawn? Can you remember when you last stretched out on the green grass and watched the ever-changing pictures in the clouds?

Wouldn't you just love to relax this afternoon beside a meandering river or a lazy little stream?

H_2O is a good way to spell—*relief!*

Chapter 8

I Spell It—FAITH

At the moment our car reached the sign "College Place: City Limits" our seven-year-old, Buddy, leaned over from the back seat and jubilantly sang out, "Daddy, I'm ready for my bike!"

Months before, in a foreign country Buddy had asked for a bike. But we explained to him, "Over here a bike is too expensive! And on these roads of rambling ruts and potholes it would be too hard to learn to ride." Buddy listened to his father's explanation and accepted his suggestion, "When we get back to the States, we'll have nice sidewalks and smooth roads. Then we'll get you a shiny new bike, just the right size."

Weeks, months, and finally a couple of years passed. Busy activities crowded out thoughts of Daddy's promise, but Buddy remembered. He knew he could count on Daddy's word. Why did Buddy have faith in his father?

When Daddy left for school each morning, he gave Buddy a hug. "I'll be back at dinnertime," he'd promise. Buddy would watch the hands of the clock. As he saw them nearing noon he'd report, "Daddy will come soon." Then he'd see him coming down the path. Daddy always kept his promises.

Prior to our return to the United States, whenever we left on a vacation in the mountains of northern Luzon, Buddy would climb into the car, eager for adventure beyond our small compound. On narrow Bailey bridges we passed over deep rushing rivers, then wound up rough dirt roads around tiny hairpin curves, with a cliff dropping off on one side and a steep wall up the other. But Buddy didn't mind. He played, sang, and slept. He could trust Daddy to get him safely to our destination—and he did!

Buddy's faith in his father came from a close relationship. He talked with him. He listened to him. He learned that obedience, and sometimes patient waiting resulted in greater happiness than if he insisted on having his own way.

Oh, yes, Buddy did get his bike! He rode it to school every day for the next several years!

Do you have this kind of faith in your heavenly Father? Richard Hammill did. He frequently talked with God. He read His messages and saw Him keep His promises. He knew he could count on His love and care to the end—but when would the end come?

Interned with some 2,000 other Americans at Los Banos camp in the Philippines, his days and nights seemed to drag on endlessly. Intense yearning for release and relief tore at his mind and very sanity. Only his faith sustained him in that terrible camp. Many, constantly hungry, became discouraged, gave up, and died. Some tried to escape, only to be shot.

Hammill's weight dropped to a mere 104 pounds, but he kept looking up. He knew that God cared. When others' faith dwindled to a trickle, he buoyed them up.

Once he heard that an American invasion fleet was approaching—but then devastating disappointment! It passed them by! How much longer could they hold out?

When morale reached its lowest ebb, Dr. Hammill says, "A miracle happened." One morning he suddenly noticed a group of large planes approaching the camp.

As they passed over the camp hundreds of small black objects began to drop out. At first he thought they were bombs, but in moments he saw the great white folds of parachutes opening. Paratroops dropped on the camp! Hammill's faith flamed as he scurried for cover.

Then in the midst of all the confusion they heard another noise. He crawled the length of the barracks and looked out the front door. The paratroopers had advanced almost to the barracks. Then amphibious army vehicles called ducks arrived! "Come on, get in!" their rescuers urged.

The internees scrambled into the large amphibious vehicles, which then moved off bouncing and lurching over the rough ground of the coconut groves. When the bumping ceased, Hammill peeked out to see what was happening. Imagine his surprise to see that the tanks were churning down the middle of a long lake, the far end of which the American army held.

As they landed a shout of relief went up!

Someday our divine Rescuer "shall send his angels with a great sound of a trumpet, and they shall gather together his elect from the four winds, from one end of heaven to the other." Matthew 24:31.

> Have faith in God—
>   Amid the battle's toll;
> Have faith in God—
>   While still the tempests roll;
> Have faith in God—
>   His peace shall keep thy soul.
> Have faith, dear friend, in God.
>   —H. M. S. Richards

Friends, the reward of your faith in Him will spell—
Ultimate Relief!